Who Bag Open?

Open?

Henry Martin

For my beautiful grandchildren.
Oliver, Verity and Darcy who give me so much
pleasure through their childish innocence.

Introduction

Idiots have two things in common. Firstly, they appear without warning and ambush you. Secondly, they all seem to follow me. Well okay, maybe not all of them follow me, but certainly a fair number of them seem to live nearby, because it seems that wherever I go, I find idiots. To be fair, most of the time they are quite harmless, at least that is they're harmless to anyone other than themselves, but they can be so frustrating and sometimes I find myself feeling tempted to put them all in a sack with a couple of bricks for ballast then toss it into the local canal.

Okay, maybe that's a bit extreme and of course murder is a crime so I'm unlikely to actually do it. Also, to be truthful, many idiots are actually quite entertaining, so when I find myself exasperated I just mentally deposit my idiots into an imaginary bag to keep them out of harm's way and this system has served me very well for many years. However, one day I found myself wondering just how many idiots I have collected in my bag over those years and that in turn led to me wondering what would happen if all the nutters managed to get out of my hypothetical bag. What would life be like if they somehow escaped and I had to meet them all again, one after the other?

The result of my pondering is this small book. It is an anthology of short tales relating how I imagine a single week in my life might be if the day ever comes when I am forced to confront the idiot apocalypse.

The day when I find myself asking; "Who left the bag of idiots open?"

The Idiot Schoolboy

Monday 08:30

I arrived at the corner shop, selected my usual daily newspaper and took it to the counter to pay the new assistant, whom I knew from a previous conversation with the owner was his niece and who was helping him out on her summer break from university. As I approached the counter a very rude schoolboy, aged about thirteen, rushed in, barged past me and demanded, "Quick, give me a paper clip".

The young lady smiled at me past the boy and politely said, "Is that all, sir? That'll be one pound forty please".

The boy interjected even more rudely, "Hey, I was first".

The young lady smiled at me again, this time apologetically, then addressed the boy, "This gentleman was first, wait just a minute please". She turned her attention back to me as I proffered my two-pound coin.

The boy started in again, "I only want a bloody paper clip and I'm in a rush 'cos my bus is coming. Just give me a paper clip and I'll go".

The young lady looked at me, realised that I wasn't in a great hurry and also recognised that I, too, thought this young man was extremely rude. She spoke slowly; "We don't have any paper clips. Only metal ones" and she smiled what I think must have been her biggest sarcastic smile at him.

"Ha ha," said the boy, "Very funny. You know what I mean".

"Oh", replied the assistant, "Do you mean one of these?" and she held up a large wire paper clip.

"That's it", said the boy. "That'll do".

"Well, you'll find them on the shelf over there. They are 99p a box".

"WHAT?" ejaculated the cretin schoolboy, "I don't want a whole box full, I only want one."

"I'm sorry, but we don't sell them singly", said the girl.

"But I haven't got 99p. Why can't you give me that one?" asked the boy, pointing at the clip which she had shown him.

"Because it doesn't belong to me", she said, "And it would be more than my job is worth to give the shop owner's property away".

I was beginning to enjoy the exchange when the lad adopted an attitude even more abrasive then before and said in an exaggerated and aggressive manner, "Oh and your wonderful job is so special and earns you so much money that would be a real tragedy if you lost it, wouldn't it!"

The lovely young lady didn't even blink before replying quite coolly, "It isn't me that hasn't got 99p for a box of paper clips. You'd better hurry up because there's your bus just pulling up. Goodbye!"

The boy turned his head and spied the bus

then ran, without a further word, out of the shop and chased the bus as it pulled away from the bus stop. As the rude boy rushed out of the shop the young assistant returned to me completely unruffled with a beaming smile and apologised for the incident, thanked me for being patient, took my two-pound coin and gave me my 60p change. She then picked up the paper clip which she had shown the boy, looked at it and smiled as she tossed it in the bin.

I thought to myself, here endeth the first lesson in how to deal with idiots and I smiled all the way home.

My Idiot Mother

Monday 11:45

I had finished reading the news and feature pages of my Daily Telegraph and I'd completed the crossword in under twenty minutes, so I decided to pour myself another cup of coffee before settling down with the sports pages when the phone in the kitchen rang. None of my friends ever calls me on my home phone and I don't use it for business, so I knew it had to be one of two things; either someone in a call centre was going to tell me that I they had all my loan history spanning the last ten years and had calculated that I was eligible to claim back several thousand pounds in overpaid Payment Protection Insurance premiums, thereby transforming my miserable and worthless life; or it was my mum. My mum always calls me on my home phone because she doesn't have a mobile phone herself and she refuses to engage with anyone else's. She bases her decision for this on the fact that the schoolchildren whom use her local bus service all seem to own mobile phones and put their feet on the bus seats, so it seems as if her reasoning is that bad behaviour is an integral part of owning a mobile phone. God knows what she thinks of me for owning two mobiles; one English and one Spanish, but they are actually the cheapest way for me to keep in touch with my European contacts. Mobile phones aside, my mum is slowly becoming more interested in technology and she has now got herself a computer. It was my mum on the phone, with a question about her new PC. I poured a coffee from the pot on the hotplate and sat on the kitchen stool whilst my mum related her morning's activity thus far which included washing and shopping and talking to her neighbour before deciding to play scrabble on her new PC. She eventually got around to telling me that the screen was so bright that it was hurting her eyes and she wanted me to remind her how to turn down the brightness. She told me she was sitting at the desk in her spare bedroom and was ready for me to tell her now.

I had already realised that the Telegraph sport section would have to wait for a bit while I talked my mum through her PC issues and the conversation went something like this:

Me: "OK mum, you need to right-click on the desktop."

Mum: "OK. Done that."

Me: "What does it say in the pop-up menu?"

Mum: "What pop-up menu?"

Me: "Didn't you get a pop-up menu?"

Mum: "No."

Me: "OK. right-click again. Do you see a pop-up menu now?"

Mum: "No."

Me: "Alright, what have you done up until

this point?"

Mum: "You told me to write 'click' and I wrote 'click'. You told me to write it again so I did. Now I've got 'click' written twice on the pad in front of me."

Me: (face palm) "Put the kettle on mum, I'll be there in an hour."

I replaced the receiver, poured my fresh coffee into the sink and looked a longing goodbye at my Telegraph, still lying open at the sport pages. Hopefully some of it would still be news when I returned from mum's house later in the day.

An idiot drunk

Monday 12:40

My mum doesn't live very far from me but I usually drive to her house, partly because I try to time my visits for when she needs shopping and particularly when she needs a "big shop" and I take her to Waitrose, but if I'm honest it's also partly because in common with many car drivers, I'm lazy. I do however like travelling on public transport, so with no shopping responsibility on this pleasant day and with the sun shining, I decided to get the bus there and perhaps enjoy a leisurely walk back. I chucked a lightweight summer jacket on, checked I had my glasses, keys, wallet etc. and set off in the direction of the bus stop.

There was a chap at the bus stop who I thought looked a little bit worse for wear and I wondered at first if he was ill, but as I approached to offer him assistance the smell of alcohol told me he had been drinking. Half ten in the morning is a bit early for me to imbibe alcohol, however some people may have their own reasons for doing so and I was pondering what might have been this chap's reason when the number 47 bus arrived. The chap was polite and stood back, gesturing quite exaggeratedly for me to board first, to which I thanked him and did so. I flashed my pass and sat on the seat on the pavement side, behind the luggage rack and the tipsy guy got on behind me, paid his fare in cash then sat on the long seat behind the driver.

It's against bus company rules to allow intoxicated people on buses and as the driver became aware of his mistake, presumably from the fumes now drifting toward him in the confines of the bus interior, he clearly wanted to distance himself from the drunk and spoke over his shoulder to ask if he might prefer to ride upstairs, pointing out that the view up there was much better. The guy rose and the driver held the bus at the stop whilst he made his way upstairs. The driver then smiled at me and pulled away.

After two stops the driver waited even though there was nobody wanting to get on or off the bus and after a minute or so of looking intently into his periscope mirror he turned and looked at the base of the stairs as the drunk reappeared, coming gingerly down and retaking his seat opposite me. The driver, clearly as bemused as I was, enquired if there was anything wrong with the upper seats, to which the drunk replied that they were fine seats and the view was indeed a good one, as promised, but he had come back down, feeling it was too dangerous to travel upstairs because there wasn't a driver up there. The driver and I exchanged a smile and he rolled his eyes before pulling away. The next stop was outside the Cricketers Arms and as we pulled in and the doors opened the drunk looked up and made what appeared to be a snap decision to visit the Cricketers and got off the bus, much to the driver's relief. I don't like drunkenness generally, but there's something about a good natured drunk that appeals to the idiot watcher in all of us isn't there?

An idiot magician

Monday 14:45

Mum's computer problem was an easy fix and it took me less than five minutes, so we spent about an hour chatting over coffee before I started on my planned walk home. As I stepped out of the front door an ambulance pulled up and the paramedics were greeted and let into next door by mum's neighbour, John.

Now I'm as nosey as the next person so I decided to hang on for a bit and see if I could find out what was going on. We watched the paramedics go in with a couple of medical bags and after about fifteen minutes they came out smiling and drove away with the whole family waving them off. As the ambulance disappeared and John's wife Maureen shepherded the twin boys back into the house, I caught John's eye and started a conversation along the lines of, "I couldn't help noticing the ambulance mate. Nothing serious I hope?"

John grinned and came to the fence so I walked a few paces to meet him there.

"Great people those paramedics", he said. "Brilliant with the kids".

"Indeed", I said, "Which one was it?"

"Both", he replied and proceeded to tell me that the family had just finished their lunch and he and Maureen were in the kitchen washing up the dishes when one of the boys, Tommy, started crying loudly and hysterically. Fearing the worst, both parents rushed into the dining room only to discover that the twins had opened Maureen's purse and had tipped the contents out. As they tried to understand the situation the parents quizzed both boys and managed to extract that at some point during their game young Tommy had placed a five pence coin in his mouth and had accidentally swallowed it. Clearly too young to fully understand his actions, Tommy was nevertheless aware enough to know that it wasn't normal to eat money and he became frightened that he would die. No amount of soothing talk could change his mind but John had a brainwave when he spotted another five pence coin in Maureen's change. He picked up the coin and palmed it, said a few hocus pocus words to enhance the magic and pretended to remove the coin from Tommy's ear. John's trick worked and had the desired effect in stopping Tommy crying as both the twins were absolutely delighted with this apparent magic. In fact the trick was so good and it impressed Terry, the other twin so much that he was jealous of his brother, so to even things up he had reached out and snatched the coin from his father's hand and swallowed it before they could stop him, then cheerfully demanded, "Do it again, do it again!"

Fortunately there was one more five pence coin, so John repeated his magic trick, then he explained to both boys that the trick would only ever work once on each of them, so they must be careful never to swallow any more coins, or indeed any other foreign objects!

The parents although not unduly worried, had thought it better to be safe than sorry and had called the ambulance to check out the boys. The paramedics had assured them that that the coins would eventually reappear, although not quite so magically and definitely from a different orifice than either of the twins' ears.

I didn't envy them their search to make sure.

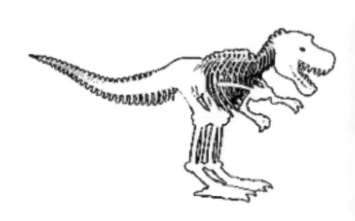

My Idiot Neighbour

Tuesday 09:15

I started Tuesday in my customary way with a short, brisk walk to the corner shop to collect my newspaper. As I walked back I met my neighbour Stacey with her six year old son Billy waiting at the school bus stop and I wished them a cheery good morning, to which they both responded. I remarked that they were a bit late for going to school and Billy was clearly excited, hardly containing himself as he proudly showed me a green plastic dinosaur and told me that they were going on a school outing to see the real dinosaurs at the Natural History Museum. I asked him what his favourite dinosaur was and he told me he that liked the Tyrannosaurus Rex best because it was the most ferocious of all the dinosaurs. He positively beamed as he described it being bigger than a double-decker bus and told me that it had such a big mouth that it could eat two grown up people like me in a single bite. Wondering at whether it was actually healthy for a six year old to be quite so enthusiastic about such gory detail I asked if he liked any smaller dinosaurs and was quite pleasantly surprised when he told me about the Pakicetus, which he described as a furry and cuddly animal about the same size as a Great Dane dog. He clearly was something of an expert and I was quite impressed by his knowledge of dinosaurs, until he added that his mum had said he could have one as a pet one day. I laughed at the innocence of children and glanced at Stacey but I stopped laughing when I saw that she wasn't smiling.

I wouldn't normally think of spoiling a six-year-old's dream, but I was so surprised to see the serious look on Stacey's face that the words were out of my mouth before I could even think about what I was saying;

"But dinosaurs are extinct!" I blurted.

"I know," said Stacey.

"So how can Billy have one as a pet if they don't exist anymore?" I said.

"Well they might bring them back."

Somewhat surprised, I said, "I don't think that's very likely, Stacey."

"Why not?" She asked.

"Because all the dinosaurs died out" I said. "That's what extinct means."

"I know that," she replied, "But they won't be extinct any more if they do bring them back again."

"Well," I said, "When something is extinct it means that there aren't any more of them anywhere in the world."

"Yeah, I know they were extinct once," said Stacey, "But that was millions of years ago and there might be some that aren't still extinct now."

I was grateful for the school bus arriving at that moment and smiled at them as they both got on, Billy rushing to sit at the back with his mates while Stacey sat at the front in one of the seats allocated for parent helpers. I waved to them as the bus drove away and I sincerely hoped that their trip to the museum would be fun, but more than that I hoped Billy would learn the meaning of extinction.

I thought it was probably a bit late for Stacey to learn, but after that conversation I also wondered if I had just learned a little more about why some species actually become extinct.

WANTED

PRAWO JAZDY

Idiot Cops

Tuesday 11:15

My girlfriend, Rosa, is also my agent and it sometimes happens that work circumstances conspire to separate us for a few days. The coming weekend was one such occasion with Rosa attending a literary agent's convention in Edinburgh and myself engaged for book signing in Swansea, so we had arranged to meet for lunch then spend the rest of the week together. We tend to linger over lunch with a few glasses of wine and of course I never drink and drive so I walked to my local taxi office, where I was greeted by Wojcek, the Polish owner, who told me that a cab would be available shortly, so I sat down to wait.

A couple of minutes later two police officers came in, saying they would like to speak to the owner about someone who they thought might be one of his drivers. The cops explained that one their station clerks had been routinely processing traffic reports and had noticed that a foreign motorist had been stopped and spoken to about committing a number of minor traffic offences in the local area approximately a dozen times in the preceding month. The police didn't consider any of the offences to be serious enough to prosecute, however the clerk had raised concern that the driver might be guilty of something more serious as he had given a different address every time he had been stopped.

Wojcek confirmed that he was the owner of the taxi firm and that he was Polish but he produced his own British driving licence and informed the officer that he had lived in England for many years and had taken the British driving test ten years previously. The first policeman asked him if he had any other Polish people working for him and Wojcek confirmed that he did indeed employ three more Poles, as well as half a dozen English drivers. The cop then showed Wojcek a sheet of paper with two words written on it and asked him if he knew the name. Wojcek's eyes flicked up from the paper to the officer's face then back to the paper. He looked at the other officer and a small smile started to appear on his face. I watched as his smile grew wider and eventually he could no longer contain the laugh that he had been suppressing.

After he stopped laughing, Wojcek slowly spoke the words, "Prawo Jazdy", before another short laugh escaped.

The officers didn't appreciate the joke and one actually became quite irritated by Wojcek's laughter and insisted that if he recognised the name he should tell the police what he knew, otherwise he might be guilty of obstructing the police in the execution of their duty.

When Wojcek saw that the irate officer was serious he laughed even more loudly and in between guffaws he managed to ask them to wait for just a moment while he delved into a drawer in the controller's desk behind the counter. After a few seconds Wojcek produced his Polish driving licence and pointed to the words at the top, explaining that 'Prawo Jazdy' is Polish for 'Driver Licence' and is printed on all Polish licences, just above the driver's name.

The officers left with slightly reddened faces and I couldn't help laughing with Wojcek as I imagined the conversation that would take place when they got back to the station.

Idiot White Van Man

Tuesday 14:50

I collected Rosa and the taxi driver dropped us in the car park of the Hillside restaurant. I paid the fare and as the taxi left Rosa took my arm, which she often does as we walk, but this time she stood still, gripped my sleeve tightly and when I looked at her she nodded towards a man who was lurching his way across the car park with keys clearly visible in his hand. The man was obviously very drunk and we both expressed surprise that he was even capable of walking, never mind driving. As we watched the man staggering around, two restaurant workers came out and stood beside us. They told us that the man had turned up drunk and tried to buy more alcohol but they refused to serve him, which made him angry and when he became aggressive they had called the police. That persuaded the man to leave but because of his very drunken state they were considering whether they should try to detain him until the cops arrived. We all agreed he probably wouldn't get very far in his condition anyway, so we watched as he climbed into his white van.

The drunk started the van and revved the engine hard before pulling forward and turning towards the car park exit on the downhill slope, where a woman in a small car was driving carefully and slowly out of the narrow exit. The drunk drove right up behind the woman's car and started flashing his headlights, repeatedly hammering on his horn and shouting at her to hurry up. This made the woman nervous and she stalled her engine, stopping the car altogether, so that the slowly rolling van came to rest against her rear bumper. Then, clearly upset at being held up, the drunk got out and staggered forward, still shouting and obviously intending to give the woman a piece of his drunken mind, but she got her car started and sensibly drove off as quickly as she could, leaving the man standing in the narrow driveway.

In his drunken state, the man had forgotten to put his handbrake on and with the woman's car now gone, his van started to slowly roll forward down the slight hill. We watched in amazement as the drunk put his arms out, first yelling at the van and ordering it to stop, then trying to hold it back physically, but of course it just kept coming.

Eventually we witnessed what looked like a slow-motion scene from a film, as the guy sank from view still waving his arms and the van rolled on over him, only stopping when it came to rest against the exit sign, with the drunk securely trapped underneath it. We were walking over to the chaos when the police car turned up.

After they ascertained that the drunk wasn't seriously hurt the officers were just as amused as we were and started to ask questions. Rosa and I gave our names and addresses but of course we had only seen a small part of the overall escapade and the restaurant staff were much more helpful, so we were allowed to continue into the restaurant, where we ordered a bottle of chilled Pinot Grigio and wondered exactly what offence the police would charge the guy with and if, indeed, it was actually an offence for an idiot to run himself over.

An Idiot Pizza Customer

Tuesday 19:15

After a lovely and long afternoon the evening eventually arrived and we took a taxi back to Rosa's flat, where a pizza delivery bike pulled up at the same time we did and the rider walked with us down the path to the block entrance. Rosa noticed the address written on the top box was that of her rude and unpleasant neighbour opposite, whom we try to avoid whenever possible; nevertheless she offered to take the pizza up to save the rider a trip. We were actually quite relieved when he thanked us but said he had to collect the money, so we shared the lift to the top floor with the delivery guy, learning as we went that his name was Simon, he was studying economics at university and was working deliveries in the evenings to support his studies, or more probably to support his social life.

When the lift doors opened Simon politely allowed us to step out first, before taking the few paces across the landing and ringing the bell on his customer's door. The door was yanked open almost immediately and the neighbour glared at us. Rosa was busily searching for her keys in her bag and didn't look up but I said "Good evening" and was pointedly ignored as the neighbour snatched the pizza boxes from Simon's hands.

Poor Simon clearly wasn't expecting such rudeness and as he held out the delivery ticket he said "Thank you for your order. There's £22.50 to pay please."

The neighbour huffed and proffered a £50 note.

Simon looked at the note for a few seconds then said, "I'm sorry but I only carry £20 in change. Do you have anything smaller please?"

The neighbour almost spat her response, "No I don't. Why don't you carry more change?"

Rosa had found her key by this time but was too busy eavesdropping like me to open the door.

Simon tried to explain, "It's about our safety", he said.

The neighbour, becoming even more obnoxious, shouted, "How is it a safety issue for delivery boys to give customers the correct change? That's stupid!"

Simon remained calm and explained further, "I sometimes go to places that aren't as nice as here and if people knew that I carried a lot of money around with me it might increase the risk of me getting robbed."

By now the neighbour was almost screaming, "So, your employer cares more about your safety than about providing good customer service?"

Visibly stunned, Simon could only offer a

weak, "Well, yes, I suppose so."

The hysterical customer screwed up the fifty pound note and threw it at Simon's feet, exclaimed at the top of her voice, "Well, that's completely stupid!" and slammed the door rudely in his face.

We watched as Simon picked up the £50 and took a deep breath. Clearly he was about to knock and attempt to reason with the neighbour from Hell, when Rosa spoke up.

"Simon!"

He looked at her sheepishly.

"Are you really studying economics?" she asked.

"Yes," he said. "Like I told you ...."

His voice trailed off as he saw Rosa's raised eyebrow and realised what she was implying. Rosa pressed the lift button and the doors opened.

"Have a nice evening", said Rosa and she smiled as Simon stepped into the lift grinning at his good fortune, courtesy of an obnoxious idiot customer.

Mother and Son Idiots

Wednesday 08:30

We woke up to a sunny morning and after a mug of freshly ground coffee we agreed to split the chores, which in reality meant me walking to the shop for milk and newspapers while Rosa made breakfast. Cornflakes, raspberry yoghurt and orange juice for her, sausage, egg, bacon and toast for me and of course, more coffee. The birds were singing in the trees, the sun was shining and I had a beautiful woman cooking breakfast for me; it was just the kind of day that could easily trick you into believing it is a perfect world.

Perfect until you come across your first idiot of the day that is.

As I returned from the paper shop the delicious smell of fried bacon wafted down to greet me. It was followed immediately by the aroma of fresh coffee and the wonderful mixture whetted and sharpened my appetite exquisitely.

As I waited for the lift I closed my eyes, lifted my head and took a deep breath in through my nose to savour the smell of my breakfast and when I reopened my eyes Terry Jones, the six-year-old lad from the flat beneath Rosa's, was standing beside me, also waiting for the lift.

Dressed in his pyjamas, Terry had a dirty face and filthy fingers and I felt the need to ask him what he'd been up to. I immediately wished I hadn't, because he beamed a big grubby smile up at me and informed me that he had learned at school the previous day that French people eat snails, so he had just been outside to try them for himself. My mind raced over all the basic biology I knew and I recalled reading somewhere that snails weren't poisonous, so in the absence of any sensible response to his statement I asked lamely, "What do they taste like?"

Again I promptly regretted my question as Terry cocked his head thoughtfully to one side for a second or two before answering, "A bit like worms."

The lift stopped at the fifth floor and Terry got out, thankfully sparing me from any further details about his unsavoury breakfast, as I was rapidly losing my appetite for my own. Terry's mum was waiting for him and she exclaimed her displeasure in no uncertain terms when she saw the state of him.

We had just sat down for breakfast and I was telling Rosa the tale of Terry and the snails when the doorbell rang. Rosa answered the door to be greeted by Terry's mum, who had come up to ask if Rosa had any ant killer. Rosa said she didn't possess any, but asked why she wanted it. Mrs Jones proceeded to explain that in addition to eating snails Terry had also swallowed a number of ants. Rosa and I exchanged concerned glances as the woman continued to tell us that she planned to give Terry a dose of ant powder to kill the ants, in addition to the slug pellets which she had already given him to make sure the snails were dead.

Rosa took the woman back downstairs to her own flat, attempting to explain that whilst the insects themselves probably weren't dangerous, the pest control pellets and powder were highly toxic and Terry would need to see a doctor immediately. Meanwhile I phoned for an ambulance and reflected that idiots do indeed breed more idiots.

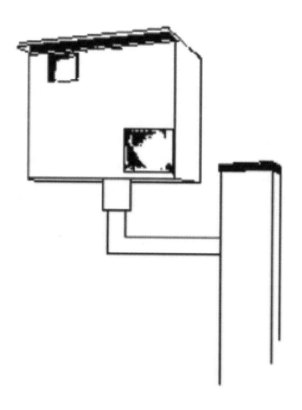

An Idiot Driver

Wednesday 11:40

The paramedics determined that Terry hadn't swallowed very much of the slug poison, which they said was quite mild anyway and they were confident of a happy outcome, so as they took him off for a thorough check-up at the hospital, we went back to Rosa's flat. Of course our breakfast had spoiled by then, so we scraped the remains into the bin, washed the dishes and started out towards the town centre, having decided to skip breakfast and go to the café for brunch instead.

Just along from Rosa's flat there is a road safety camera which protects the public by photographing any motorist who drives faster than the 30mph limit. As we approached the camera a car came toward us travelling at what appeared to be reasonable speed, but the camera flashed twice as the car passed it so we assumed that the driver must have been just over the speed limit. The car screeched to a halt and remained still for a minute, then started reversing back the way it had just come. We watched it travel about a hundred yards or so before it stopped, then started forward again, accelerating until it passed the speed camera a second time. Again there were two flashes and again the car stopped.

We had drawn almost level with the camera by this time and we stopped walking to watch as the driver once more reversed and drove past the camera for a third time. The car was clearly within the permitted speed limit this time, but as it passed over the white painted marks on the road, sure enough the two flashes came again. This time the driver stopped and reversed back only about thirty yards before creeping forward at little more than walking speed. The camera flashed twice again and it became clear that it wasn't working properly.

The driver had seen us watching and he called across the road to us and explained that he was sure he had not been speeding when he was first flashed, so he had reversed back a few times just to check his theory that it was actually a malfunctioning camera. Having established that he was innocent, he was satisfied that he wouldn't receive a speeding fine in the post so he smiled and was about to drive off when a police car emerged from the side road and pulled up alongside him. The police officers asked the man to switch off his engine and step out of his car and we could hear the conversation clearly from our side of the road. The officers told the driver that they had been watching him and they asked him what he was doing, so he explained just as he had told us, that he was just confirming the camera was out of order. The officers assured him they would report the faulty camera, then one of them gave him a lecture on road safety, including the dangers of reversing further than is necessary on the road. They then told him they had noticed he wasn't wearing a seatbelt so they called him an idiot for risking his safety and a bigger idiot for drawing attention to himself whilst breaking the law and they issued him with a ticket for not wearing his seatbelt, which would cost him sixty pounds and put three points on his licence.

A Rude Idiot

Just as we finished our brunch an expensive looking German-built car pulled up outside, parked with two wheels on the pavement and the driver, wearing an expensive suit, jumped out and charged into the café, obviously in a hurry. He barged past the queue of four orderly customers before pushing in at the front and barking his order; "Two bacon sandwiches to take away and make it quick, I'm on a double-yellow."

Fred, who was taking customer's orders at the counter, looked at the guy and calmly told him he would have to wait his turn and to go to the back of the queue, at which the man raised his voice and said, "I've got an important meeting and don't have time to queue. I need my order now."

Fred addressed the man again and said, "The longer you stand there, the later you're going to be. I'm not serving you first, so go to the back of the queue."

The man was clearly agitated and asked, as if it mattered, "Who do you think you're talking to in that tone?"

Fred replied, "I don't know and I don't care. If you want to be served at all, get in the queue!"

Clearly not used to being put in his place,

the guy banged his fist on the counter and demanded, "How dare you talk to a customer like that? Get me the manager, now!"

Fred looked the guy squarely in the eye and opened his mouth as if he was going to speak, but changed his mind and let out a sigh instead. He turned and called into the kitchen, "Sally, there's someone here who wants to speak to the manager."

Sally emerged from the kitchen wiping her hands on a cloth and shot a quizzical glance at Fred before addressing the suit, "Hello, I'm the manager here. How can I help you sir?"

"That man was extremely rude to me," said the angry guy. "I think you should fire him!"

Sally replied, "I'm sorry sir, but I only manage the staff and the business and I don't have the authority to fire him."

The suit became almost apoplectic and shouted, "Rubbish! If you can't deal with this then I demand you call the owner now and I warn you, I expect to be compensated for my time dealing with this bullshit!"

Sally smiled pleasantly and said, "I'm sure you can discuss that with him, sir." Then she turned and said mildly, "Back to you Fred," and she walked behind the counter.

The suit looked from Sally to Fred then banged the counter again and said, "What the Hell is this? I want to talk to the owner of this dump."

Fred smiled his friendliest smile and said

with a twinkle in his eye, "Well that would be me sir!"

The man spluttered and eventually stormed out muttering something about taking his business elsewhere.

All the customers in the café started laughing and Sally said to Fred, "That was very mischievous of you dad, why did you have to involve me?"

"Oh, I don't know," said Fred, "I just wanted to see the look on the idiot's face when he realised I actually own this place!"

Sally rolled her eyes and went back to her kitchen.

Fred turned to the next customer and said, "I love my job. What can I get you sir?"

An Idiot Fuel Thief

Wednesday 14:30

Fred is a friend of ours and after he finished serving he brought a fresh pot of coffee over and sat with us for a chat.

Fred and his wife Maggie loved camping holidays, but when they reached their sixties they found erecting tents started to be harder work so they had recently invested in a motorhome and had sensibly spent the previous weekend at a fairly local campsite, getting to know their new camper before taking it further afield. It seems they weren't the only ones who were unfamiliar with their new vehicle and Fred told us this tale.

After arriving at the campsite on Friday afternoon, Fred and Maggie were directed to the service area, where they filled their fresh water tank and were shown where to pump out their waste tank, which they planned to do before leaving the following Tuesday morning. Then they parked up in their allotted space, plugged into the electric supply and settled down to enjoy a cup of tea.

They were pleased at not having to wrestle with guy ropes and ground pegs in the mud but as they had got older they had both been making more frequent nocturnal visits to the smallest room and they agreed that the most pleasant advantage of the camper was that they no longer had to traipse across the campsite to use the communal facilities.

Always on the lookout for ideas to improve their own business, Maggie and Fred like to visit other restaurants, so on the Friday night they ate an Indian curry; on Saturday they had a Thai meal and on Sunday it was Chinese. Unfortunately the spicy mixture gave them both a mild touch of diarrhoea on the Monday, making them even more appreciative of their personal toilet.

Fred got up to use the toilet about two am on Tuesday morning and as he flushed it he was startled by some unexpected sounds from outside. The first was a loud whoosh, the second was a muffled cough and there was a crash of somebody falling over. He looked out of the widow and saw a man, soaking wet, covered in filth and writhing uncontrollably on the ground. The man's screams awoke the whole of the campsite and alerted the site security patrol who immediately understood what had happened and telephoned the police.

It turned out that for couple of months the man had been systematically stealing diesel from the campers parked on the site by inserting a plastic tube into the fuel tank and sucking slowly on the other end until the laws of physics took over and the syphoning process continued automatically. On this occasion, working in the dark, he had mistaken Fred's waste tank outlet valve for the fuel tank and had been attempting to suck at the exact same time as Fred had flushed the toilet. The electric flush pump had discharged several litres of diarrhoea straight up the syphoning tube and sprayed the thief from head to toe with a mixture of exotic effluent.

Fred made a statement to assist the police with prosecution of course, but he told us that he almost felt sorry for doing so because when all was said and done he thought that poetic justice had been served to the idiot thief and the incident had actually given him the best laugh he'd had in a long time.

An Idiot Plumber and his Mate

Thursday 10:00

Rosa had a slight leak under her bathroom basin and had booked a plumber to come and look at it that morning so we had breakfast, cleared the dishes, made a fresh pot of coffee and settled down to await his arrival.

The doorbell rang and I answered it to find a plumber and a small boy aged about four. The plumber explained that the boy was his son, who's pre-school had declared a "Baker Day" and was closed to pupils while teachers did some teambuilding. His wife was visiting her mother who had fallen ill suddenly and the plumber hoped we didn't mind him bringing young Toby with him, assuring us that he was well behaved and wouldn't be in the way. What can one say, except okay?

We offered the plumber coffee and Toby orange juice and both were accepted, so I prepared the drinks whist Rosa showed the plumber the problem. He had a quick look and said that the cold water connector needed replacing. He estimated thirty minutes work and said he could fix it there and then, to which Rosa happily agreed.

After about fifteen minutes the plumber came out of the bathroom looking a bit green and asked if he could have some water from the kitchen tap. We offered him more coffee and he thanked us but declined, saying it was water he needed. We directed him to the kitchen and watched as he filled the mug, drank, swilled it around his mouth and spat it into the sink. He did this several times before finally swallowing some of the water, then asking if it would, after all, be possible to have some coffee. We pointed at the pot and he helped himself. Toby was standing by the kitchen door looking quite sheepish and we must clearly have looked bemused, so the plumber explained.

He was lying on his back with his head under the basin while trying to tighten a nut when Toby tapped his arm and told him that he had made him a drink and presented him with some water in the mug. Apparently this is a game that Toby likes to play at home, so there seemed nothing unusual in it. The plumber drank the water, gave the mug back to Toby and went back to tightening his fitting. Almost immediately Toby had presented his dad with another drink and again the plumber drank it down and gave the mug back. When he started to tighten the fitting again he felt a third tap on his arm and as he looked at Toby the thought occurred to him that he had turned off the water in the bathroom to carry out his repair and Toby certainly hadn't had time to get to the kitchen and back. Then he spied the toilet seat up, put two and two together and realised that Toby had been dipping the mug into the toilet to fill it.

We couldn't help laughing but Rosa assured him that the toilet was clean and that there were no chemicals added to the cistern. Then she kept Toby occupied while the plumber finished his work.

He refused to accept any more than a nominal payment and we doubted that he would be idiot enough to take a four-year-old plumber's mate with him on any more jobs!

The First Idiot Cashier

Thursday 14:30

I love playing blues on guitar and I had been considering buying a blues harp for some time, to augment my playing, so after lunch Rosa suggested that we went for a stroll and popped into the music shop to get some advice and of course I readily agreed. For clarification, a blues harp is a type of harmonica and it shouldn't be confused with that magnificent Irish stringed frame that is more akin to the inside of a piano.

The assistant was a really knowledgeable and helpful guy called Derek, who even produced his own harp and played a bit for me to demonstrate how various techniques are employed to vary notes and tones and to emphasise that playing a harp requires far more than just blowing and sucking. He mounted several harps, one at a time, onto a kind of bellows frame which demonstrated the difference in tone between harps of different keys. I learnt a lot about cross-harping and various other applications from Derek. I also learnt the names of some great harp players and I even discovered some music which I wasn't previously aware of. It was a very enjoyable experience and although I knew that to be a serious harp player I would eventually need a selection of harps in all keys, I decided to start with two, one in the key of C because that's the key that most instruction manuals seem to use for teaching and one in A, so that I could jam a bit, crossharping with my friends who play a lot of blues in E.

I thanked Derek and took my purchases to the checkout desk, where Derek had assured me that Damian would be happy to take my money.

I handed over my purchases, Damian put them in a carrier bag, told me the price and I offered my credit card. Damian apologised and informed me that the phone line was down so the card payment machine was out of order, which prompted me to offer to go and withdraw cash from an ATM at the bank across the street, but Damian didn't want to trouble me and insisted he was too clever to be thwarted by a breakdown in technology. He reached into a cupboard and retrieved an old fashioned rollover machine, which mechanically recorded the details on my card onto a special slip and required me to sign the slip to authorise the transaction. I was signing the slip when Damian noticed that I had never signed my name on the back of my credit card. He informed me that he couldn't complete the transaction unless the card was signed and explained that it was necessary for him to compare the signature on the credit card with the signature I signed on the purchase slip, so I borrowed Damian's pen and signed the credit card in front of him. He then proceeded to study both signatures, carefully comparing the one I had just signed on the card with the one I had just signed on the purchase slip. Fortunately for me Damian pronounced that the two signatures did indeed match and he was therefore happy to complete the transaction and let us leave the shop with my purchases.

Rosa and I looked at each other in amazement then left the shop and headed for home by the shortest route, hoping to avoid meeting any more Damians.

The Second Idiot Cashier
(and her idiot manager)

Thursday 18:30

We enjoyed a long afternoon walking in
the park and worked up an appetite but we
didn't fancy cooking, so we took the long
way home, passing a well-known fast food
restaurant. I fancied a cheeseburger and
fries with coffee and Rosa wanted a chicken
burger with no dressing and fries with a
juice. We queued at the desk for about
fifteen minutes, wondering more than once
why it was called fast food, until we were
eventually greeted by a huge smile beneath
an even huger cap.

We ordered our burgers and were told we
would have to wait for the chicken, which
pleased Rosa as the very reason she orders
it without dressing is to ensure that it is
freshly cooked and hasn't been kept warm
for ages. We asked if we could leave the
rest of the order until the chicken was
cooked, so it would all be hot at the same
time. This request must have switched
something off under the cap, because Huge-
smile informed us that this wasn't possible.
We explained that we always did this and it
had never been a problem before, so Huge-
smile went off to check with a deputy

manager.

The deputy manager listened to Huge-smile then came and told us, grudgingly, that he would agree to delay serving the other items, as long as we paid for the meals in full in advance, which we considered normal procedure and were of course happy to do.

After punching till buttons for a few moments Huge-smile told us that our bill would be £9.16. Rosa had already calculated this and handed Huge-smile a ten pound note and sixteen pence in coins. Huge-smile faded and became Half-smile.

Half-smile advised Rosa, "You've given me too much money."

"I know", replied Rosa, "So that you can give me a one-pound coin back."

Half-smile became Grimace and advised us that the deputy manager's advice would have to be obtained on yet another difficult decision.

The deputy manager listened intently once more to Grimace before advising us that it wasn't restaurant policy to "do that sort of thing" and that we would have to pay the exact amount or accept the correct change.

I laughed but Rosa shot me a sideways glance then proceeded to explain to the deputy manager that the proffered £10.16 minus the cost of £9.16 left an even one pound, which avoided her having too many coins in her purse. The deputy manager reiterated that it wasn't possible to change restaurant policy and walked off. Grimace returned to Half-smile.

By this time even Rosa, normally imperturbable, looked exasperated as she held out her hand to receive her sixteen pence back.

The chef shouted that the chicken-no-dressing was ready, so Half-smile packed our order, handed us a bag and a drinks tray then accepted Rosa's ten pound note and gave her back one pound and eighty four pence.

I saw that Rosa was about to point out that we had now actually been undercharged by a pound, so I took her arm and led her away from the counter, not because I am dishonest, but I really did want to eat my burger while it was still hot!

We put the pound in a charity box and concluded our earlier discussion by agreeing that the reason it was called fast food was probably because no matter how long it took, the staff were definitely even slower.

Memories of an Idiot Librarian

Thursday evening

We got back to Rosa's flat and she went to "slip into something more comfortable" while I poured us drinks and selected some music from her extensive collection of blues albums, which includes rare stuff by artists including Kitty Brown and Ivory Joe Hunter as well as contemporary musicians like Robert Cray and Eric Clapton.

Rosa is such a big fan of the blues that during the final hours of her maternity labour thirty years earlier, she had blues playing in the delivery suite and B.B. King's "There Must Be A Better World Somewhere" was playing at the very moment she gave birth to a beautiful baby girl. The musical influence and the overwhelming emotion combined with the gas and air she had been using and Rosa immediately named her daughter B.B. after the great man himself; an incongruous choice for a girl as B.B. is a hypocoristic abbreviation of the nickname, "Blues Boy".

Whoever B.B. meets usually assumes that her name is Bibi, or Bebe and comments that it is quite an unusual name, whereupon she enjoys telling them the story of how she got her even more unusual real name, because of the music playing at the precise moment she made her entry into the world. Most people find the explanation interesting and thereafter call her B.B. or just B. Rosa and I, however, often use a different name for her.

When B.B. passed her A levels with four straight 'A's she was thrilled to be offered a place at a top university to study for a joint BA Honours degree in English Literature and German language. Upon registering at her first day at the university, which I think would prefer to remain anonymous, B.B. dutifully filled out numerous forms for refectory pass, student union membership, gymnasium membership and library card, among many other things. Everything went well enough until she visited the library with her induction tour group and the clerk informed her that initials were not acceptable on library documents and asked her to write her full name on the application form. B.B. explained, telling her usual story, that B.B. is actually her name and not her initials, but the clerk was unimpressed and informed her that they 'did things properly' at this university and reiterated that abbreviations were unacceptable. The clerk was adamant, saying that she understood B.B.'s wish to be known by a pseudonym but insisted she would need to make this clear on her application form. After a short and fruitless discussion B.B. noticed that the group was moving on and she didn't want to be left behind, so she quickly took the clerk's pen and wrote on her application form, making it as clear as she thought she could, B only B only. This seemed to satisfy the clerk who then took the form with a smile and B.B. hurried along to catch up with her group.

Later in the week she went to the student administration office to collect her paperwork, including her new library membership and was amazed to see that the card had been issued with her photograph in the name of, Bonly Bonly.

B.B. decided that it just wasn't worth the time and effort to explain again, so she used that card for four years in the name of Bonly Bonly and Rosa and I had called her Bonly ever since.

I don't think she has ever forgiven the idiot at the library.

When Idiots Fly

Friday 07:30

It was an early start to catch Rosa's Edinburgh flight, so we decided to have breakfast at the airport. We awoke at 04:00 and I made coffee whilst she packed her overnight bag, then we showered, drank another coffee and I drove us to the airport in her car. Rosa only had hand luggage, so we parked in the short-stay area and headed straight for the restaurant near end of the departure lounge. On our way we checked the screens for flight information and noticed incidentally that an earlier flight to Aberdeen had been delayed.

We enjoyed a full English and coffee which was spoilt only by the chap on the next table who was annoyed about the delayed flight to Aberdeen and who made several loud telephone calls throughout our meal, informing just about everyone he knew that he was delayed and telling them what he thought of the airline. We gathered that he was some kind of drilling manager who had to catch a connecting helicopter to one of the offshore oil rigs and was worried he would miss his connection.

As we finished our breakfast the tannoy sounded its familiar 'bing-bong' then a pleasant female voice apologised for the delay to passengers for Aberdeen and announced that the flight was finally boarding. The voice also announced that Rosa's flight would be boarding shortly, so we made our way toward the domestic flights gate and joined the queue.

The oilman had walked straight to the front and was demanding that the staff allow him on the plane first as he had already been significantly inconvenienced and he was considering taking legal action against the airline. He must have felt a bit silly when the steward allowed him to finish his rant before informing him loudly, so that we could all hear, that he was at gate fifteen for Edinburgh and that the Aberdeen gate was sixteen. He stormed across to the correct gate and started to repeat his demands but he got a pretty cool reception from the girl at the desk who informed him that he would have to join the queue. The oilman puffed out his chest, repeated his demand to be allowed on first and added, "Do you have any idea who I am?"

The young lady leaned forward to her microphone, pressed a button which triggered the familiar 'bing-bong' and her voice came over the air loud and clear, "Attention please. There is a gentleman attempting to board the Aberdeen flight who doesn't appear to know who he is. Anyone who can identify this passenger, please come to gate sixteen. Thank you."

The announcement made everyone in both queues laugh, except for the oilman who was incensed and by this time had attracted the attention of two security guards who were quickly approaching gate sixteen.

The young lady said "I'm sorry sir, but you will have to queue up, just like everybody else."

The oilman, clearly at the end of his tether finally blew his cool altogether and shouted at her, "Screw you!"

As the security guards took the man's arms the girl beamed a huge smile at him and nodded at one of the security men, before saying, "You'll have to queue up for that as well, behind my boyfriend, who is currently holding your right arm!"

I have never seen an obnoxious idiot shut up quite so quickly.

Idiot Sailors

Friday 08:40

After Rosa's flight took off I decided to kill a bit of time and try to avoid the morning rush hour traffic before starting my drive to Swansea, so I went back to the restaurant for another coffee. I sat at a table near the entrance and shortly afterwards the two security guys, who were having a well-earned break after dealing with the idiot oilman, came and sat at the table next to mine and we got chatting about the incident and other things. The boyfriend told me that the obnoxious oilman had been cautioned about his behaviour and they had detained him until the very last minute before releasing him with just enough time to run and catch his flight, to try and teach him some manners.

Despite both being built like brick outhouses and clearly very tough cookies, both of the guards were pleasant and easy-going and said that handling exceptionally rude people was 'all in a day's work' and that they dealt with obnoxious people like the oil idiot half a dozen times a day. In fact they were almost bemoaning the fact that such people were just boring and that there were no really interesting or entertaining idiots these days. Then the other guard recalled an interesting idiot story.

He told us that he used to work on the oil drilling platform helicopter ferry pads in Scotland and he said that each helicopter carries two inflatable life rafts, just in case they ever needed to come down in the sea in an emergency. Apparently one day some really dangerous idiot employees decided to steal one of the inflatable rafts, potentially putting people's lives at risk of course. Now, security arrangements are very stringent at the helipads, so it must have taken a fair bit of ingenuity and detailed planning to detach the life raft and get it out of the helicopter, smuggle it through the security gate and drive it all the way up the coast to Inverness, where they attempted to sell it to a local fisherman.

Their plan was thwarted when the fisherman asked for a trial run and they took the raft out on the Moray Firth to demonstrate its seaworthiness. They happily bobbed along for twenty minutes or so, putting the inflatable through its paces, showing the fisherman just how sturdy the boat was and demonstrating all of its capabilities, when they were disturbed by a red and white helicopter hovering about a hundred feet above them. No matter what they did, the helicopter wouldn't go away and eventually they decided to return to the harbour. Nobody knows whether the fisherman would actually have bought the boat or not because when they arrived back on dry land they were met by officers of Her Majesty's Coastguard, accompanied by a sergeant and three constables from Burnett Road Police Station in Inverness.

The fisherman made a statement and was released while the idiots were arrested and later charged with several offences, including theft of the life raft and wasting HM Coastguard's time.

The idiot sailors might have got away with their theft if it hadn't been for the fact that when they launched the boat it automatically triggered a distress signal and the helicopter that had been hovering over them was a Search and Rescue helicopter that had locked on to the signal and homed in on the life-raft.

No entry for heavy
goods vehicles.
Residential site only

←

Nid wyf yn y swyddfa
ar hyn o bryd. Anfonwch
unrhyw waith i'w gyfieithu.

An Idiot Signwriter

Friday 13:10

When the London rush hour traffic had cleared a bit I started out on the drive to Swansea which I knew was going to be the most enjoyable three hours driving I had done in a long time. Rosa didn't really like driving the red 1960 MK 2 Jaguar which her dad had left to her, but I loved it and I was always glad to remind her that it needed a run once in a while to keep everything moving freely. I eased the beautiful motor car on to the M4 and the powerful 3.8 litre engine purred its way up to seventy miles an hour.

After an uneventful and thoroughly enjoyable drive I arrived in Swansea and headed for the front, driving by the dock area, along Oystermouth Road, past County Hall and towards my hotel. As I approached Victoria Park I came to some road works and was hailed to pull up by a man dressed in orange overalls and carrying a red 'STOP' sign. As I put the handbrake on, the man approached the car and I wound the driver's window down to speak to him. He commented on how beautiful the car was, which I expected, then he apologised and advised me there would be a delay of approximately five minutes whilst a crane used the road to manoeuvre as it lifted out a signpost and hoisted another one in to replace it. I could see the sign being removed and it looked to me just like any other road information sign in Swansea, black lettering on a white background with English on top and Welsh below. The English wording advised that the street was residential and traffic was restricted to light traffic only with all heavy goods vehicles prohibited.

The sign looked quite new, so I asked the guy in orange overalls why it was being changed, apparently so soon after being erected. He laughed and told me that despite all being Swansea natives, none of the workers in the roads and highways department could actually read Welsh, so when they were making the sign the fabricator had emailed the English wording to a colleague in the translation department and asked for a the Welsh translation. The response came back straight away and the fabricators proceeded to make the sign accordingly. When the sign was made it was sent to the erection crew, none of whom could read Welsh either, and the sign was duly put up the next day, which was the previous Tuesday.

On the same day a Welsh speaking councillor had contacted the department and pointed out an error, which meant that the new sign had to be replaced quickly. The orange-suited guy explained that the email response from the colleague in the translation department was 'Nid wyf yn y swyddfa ar hyn o bryd. Anfonwch unrhyw waith i'w gyfieithu', which was actually an automatic out of office response that translated into English as, "I am not in the office at the moment. Your requests for translation will be dealt with later." The fabricators and erectors, unable to read Welsh, had mistaken the out-of-office automated response for the translation they had requested and had made and put up the sign with the automated response wording.

The man assured me that the new sign had been double-checked to ensure it was correctly worded and idiot proofed.

Another Drunken Idiot

Friday 20:00

After checking into my hotel I decided to stretch my legs by walking to the town centre to familiarise myself with the whereabouts of the two shops I would be signing books at the next day. I worked up a bit of an appetite on the walk so I went back to the hotel restaurant, stopping at the bar for an aperitif on the way.

I was enjoying my beer when a car pulled up outside, two wheels on the pavement and the driver came in and asked for a pint of 'Paddington Bear'. The bartender managed not to smile as he informed the man that he didn't sell Paddington Bear and asked if he meant Boddington's bitter? It took several seconds for the information to register and for the man to manipulate his mouth into shape sufficiently to respond and ask for another 'Paddington Bear' but as the bartender was about to repeat his answer a waiter walked past carrying a bottle of white wine. The sight of the wine caused the man to change his mind and he ordered a glass of 'Peanut Grigo' instead. The bartender glanced at me with a slightly raised eyebrow but still resisted the urge to smile and remained very professional as he suggested that perhaps the man had had enough to drink already.

Whilst this exchange between the drunken man and the bartender was going on a police car had pulled up outside and two policemen had entered the bar. The first policeman addressed the man and asked if he was the driver of the car outside and the man responded honestly that he was. The policemen asked him, "How long have you been drinking?" to which he replied that he had left work at lunchtime and had gone to a pub near his office with some colleagues where he had drunk, "Six or seven pints". He then said that he had started to walk back to work with a colleague but they had stopped at another pub on the way when they saw that it was advertising 'Happy Hour Cocky Tales' and he had another beer and five or six delicious drinks called "Margaret and Rita".

After their cocktails the man's colleague was a bit worse for wear so he decided to drive him home and collected his car from the firm's car park. When they arrived at his friend's home he had gone in for "A quick brandy or two, to keep out the cold." With the warming brandies inside him he decided to go home himself, stopping on the way at an off licence to buy a bottle of wine. He fumbled about inside his coat before eventually producing the now empty bottle from his pocket and handing it to the policeman. He had been sitting in the evening traffic and had become thirsty, so he had parked outside and come into the hotel bar for another drink.

Having listened patiently to the man's story, the policeman asked him for his car keys and as the drunk handed his keys over, the second cop produced a breathalyser unit and said, "I will need you to blow into this and provide a breath sample."

For the first time the drunken man showed a sign of agitation as he replied quite indignantly, "Why? Don't you believe me?"

At last the idiot drunk had made the bartender give in and smile.

Wiffy Idiots

Saturday 11:00

After a "full Welsh" breakfast on Saturday morning, I telephoned Rosa to check the details of my engagements, wish her luck with her convention speech and of course to tell her I loved her, then I walked the mile or so to my morning appointment.

The book shop was a large Victorian building, spread over three floors that had been transformed and modernised by its owner, including the addition of a "purchase library" section, where people could exchange their books once they had read them and receive a small discount against new purchases with the returned books being resold in the shop's second hand department. The idea was born out of a joint initiative with the University of Wales to help students afford the cost of their expensive textbooks, but it had become so popular that the shop had extended the service to include all people and all books.

There was also a small coffee shop, where customers could take the second hand books, free to read, whilst they drank their coffee and ate a slice of 'home-made' cake. The coffee shop also offered an hour of free internet access for customers and was therefore very popular with students and researchers who bought a fresh drink every hour.

The store manager introduced me to a young lady who would assist me throughout the morning and we were seated at a table draped with posters and piled with copies of my new book, 'Ray's story'. The table was situated between the second hand counter and the coffee shop, which as a coffee lover I found to be a particularly convenient location.

After an hour or so of fairly brisk book signing the initial small crowd had shrunk to just a few individuals and we decided it was time for a drink, so my young assistant offered to collect coffees from the shop. As she rose to go we saw that the relative calm of the coffee shop was being disturbed by a middle-aged couple who were making a bit of a fuss at the counter. The lady was berating the Barista for not giving her something she clearly thought she was entitled to and the besieged Barista was trying to placate her customer with offers of chocolate topping, a flake or marshmallows, but all to no avail. The lady was making such a fuss that the store manager arrived at the till at the same time as my assistant. The manager seemed to understand the problem immediately and she led the couple to a table near the window and sat to have a quiet word with them. After a couple of minutes the couple started to laugh and the manager seemed to be entertaining them with her smartphone, having apparently resolved the situation.

When my assistant returned with our coffee she could hardly contain her smile and she explained what had happened.

It seemed that the lady was upset because she thought she was being diddled when the Barista didn't understand her request for their free "wiffys" to go with their coffee. She had apparently seen the Free WiFi sign over the entrance and thought WiFi was a kind of cake or biscuit that was given to those customers who purchased drinks. An explanation by the manager complete with a demonstration on her smart phone along with a couple of complimentary Kit-Kats had resolved the wiffy idiot situation amicably.

A Pair of Idiot Shoplifters

Saturday 13:30

At the end of an enjoyable and reasonably profitable three hours selling and signing books I had a slight touch of writer's cramp, but was otherwise feeling very content with the results of the morning. Packing up was quick and easy because I had used more of the shop's stock of books than we had estimated we would do and far from having to take any books away I had been promised that the shop would actually be ordering more. I thanked my young assistant for her help and of course I presented her with a personalised copy of the book she had been selling all morning, then I went to the coffee shop to share an Americano with the manager and sign a few more stock copies as she had requested.

Near the entrance to the coffee shop were a couple of "Bargain Book" tables, which were loaded with old or otherwise surplus stock that the shop was selling off at a reduced price of two pounds each. People could browse and select the books they wanted then take them to a sales assistant who would verify the special deal and take the payment at the most convenient till. It was a busy area with an assortment of people as varied as the subject matter of the books and of all ages, including children.

A couple of teenaged boys, probably around sixteen years old, were hanging around the bargain tables and looking decidedly suspicious, so the manager pointed them out to me and explained that she was keeping an eye on them because she recognised the way they were wearing their jackets, open and lose, as a familiar style to that employed by shoplifters because it was easy to slip a book under their arm. She used her in-store walkie-talkie, to alert the member of staff who was assisting in the sale area and the man acknowledged then walked over to the two boys and asked them politely if there was anything he could help them with.

The boys were each holding a book and were clearly caught with their guard down by the assistant's approach to them, so one of the boys waved his book vaguely and asked, "Err, how much are these books, please?"

The assistant pointed to the sign and told him they were two pounds each and the boy nervously stuck his hand into his pocket, rummaged around and eventually produced a five pound note, which he handed sheepishly to the assistant. The assistant then asked the boys to accompany him to the till, but as he turned towards the second hand counter to take the payment, the boys' nerves broke and they panicked and ran from the shop, clutching the books as they sped off.

The boys were far too quick off the mark and much too sprightly for the assistant to have any chance of catching them but he didn't seem particularly bothered and didn't even attempt to run after them. He just watched them go then walked up to our table where the manager asked him, "Did I just watch those boys steal two books?"

The assistant grinned as he held up the five pound note and replied, "I'd say it's more like we just robbed them boss, because I very much doubt that the idiots will be coming back for their one pound change."

When Idiots Combine

My second appointment was from 2:30pm to 5:30pm in the book section of a quality independent department store. I was provided with a lovely assistant named Lucy for the gig and we were seated at a well-stocked table on the first floor, where Lucy assured me that the store wasn't making a subconscious comment about my book, because we happened to be close to the customer toilets. I laughed and to be honest I didn't mind the positioning at all because the toilets are often busy places, so with no pun intended, I thought we would be assured of a bit of 'passing trade'.

Whilst we were there a customer's child had 'an accident' in the toilets and the cleaners were called. They closed the toilets for a short period and during the interim cleaning I noticed that one of the department employees was becoming quite agitated. As I watched the lady getting increasingly more irritable it occurred to me that I had noticed her visiting the toilets every half an hour or so, although I hadn't given it too much thought until then. The anxious assistant was clearly relieved when the cleaners finished because as soon as they left she was the first visitor. However, her relief didn't last very long, because within a couple of minutes we heard the muffled 'whumph' of a small explosion, followed immediately by a scream for help.

Lucy looked at me momentarily then rushed into the toilet, closely followed by another shop assistant. Seconds later Lucy emerged and grabbed a fire extinguisher from the wall whilst simultaneously calling to me to phone for an ambulance.

I used my mobile phone to call 999 and after a few minutes managed to explain the situation as best as I could and both ambulance and fire service duly arrived about ten minutes later.

It turned out that because the cleaners had been called at short notice, on a Saturday afternoon, they had already packed up for the day and hadn't got their usual cleaning products readily available, so one of their idiot number had picked up some cleaning fluid from the hardware department, without reading the label and didn't realise that it was highly flammable. They had cleaned up the child's mess then poured the rest of the non-approved fluid into the toilet, which probably wouldn't have been a problem in normal use, but the reason for the assistant's earlier irritation was that she was an addicted smoker and her frequent visits to the toilet were so that she could have a crafty cigarette. It seems that she sat on the toilet, sparked her lighter and 'whoof', the fumes ignited.

Thanks to Lucy's quick thinking and action with the fire extinguisher the damage to the toilet was minimal and the store expected emergency repairs would have it back in use in time for Monday's opening, however the assistant wasn't so lucky and was expected to be off work for at least a week with a burnt bottom. I'd guess that she also came back to face disciplinary action over the smoking and was probably looking for a new job shortly thereafter.

All in all it was an exciting afternoon and an excellent example of what can happen when two idiots inadvertently conspire to demonstrate just how creative their combined stupidity can be.

An Idiot Complainer

Saturday 20:00

That evening in the hotel, two guests caught my attention. A young man wearing a football shirt was drinking at the bar when he was approached by an irritated middle-aged woman. Their conversation went something like this:

Her, "Excuse me, young man."

Him, "Yes?"

"Where is the concierge?"

"I don't know, sorry."

"That's not good enough. What sort of employee are you?"

"Employee? Sorry, I'm just having a beer."

"I'm going to report you!"

The young man seemed amused at this point and said, "You'll have to report me to someone wearing a hotel uniform. You'll probably find that all the real employees are wearing one."

"So you're not even wearing your uniform? You don't know where your colleagues are, you drink on duty and you don't show any respect to guests. Call the manager right now. I'm going to make a formal complaint!"

The guy turned back to his beer saying, "Would it occur to you that I might not work here?"

However the woman wasn't the type to

give up easily. "I'm not leaving until you call the manager."

The young man held his hands up and said, "Okay, I give in." Then he asked the barman to page the manager.

The barman had been eavesdropping and smiling to himself, as I had, so he called the manager and explained the situation.

The manager arrived within two minutes and said, "Hello. What appears to be the problem?"

Her, "Why do you employ people like this?" She gestured at the young man. "He isn't wearing his uniform, he has refused to help me find the concierge and he's drunk!"

Manager, "I'm sorry madam, but this gentleman isn't a hotel employee, as you can tell by the fact that he isn't wearing a hotel uniform."

"You're protecting him! You won't get away with it. I'm going to write to the Hotel owner. "

"I assure you madam; this gentleman is a guest, just like yourself. If you look around you'll notice that all the hotel employees are wearing uniforms and I'm sure any one of them would be pleased to help you."

"Well, he's not wearing his uniform and I demand you deal with him NOW!"

At this point the young man became fed up with what had started as an amusing situation but had developed into an irritation. He said, "Hey, I'll tell you what. Let's make this easy. I resign. I've had enough of this job and having to deal with stupid guests like this woman, so I'm leaving. I won't even work my notice and you can post my P45 to me."

The woman triumphantly said, "Aha, so I was right. You do work here! Well not anymore and good riddance to you." Then she turned, threw her chiffon scarf over her shoulder dramatically and marched out of the door, right past the concierge she had been looking for initially.

The manager watched the woman leave then turned to the young man, smiled and said, "It was nice being your boss for about two minutes!" Then he asked the barman for the man's bill. He looked briefly at it before saying, "As a gesture of appreciation for your valued service whilst working at the hotel we would like to provide you with a small leaving party." Then he ordered a free drink for the young man and for me, apologised for the woman's rudeness and tore up the young man's bill.

The Idiot Traffic Warden

Sunday 07:10

I checked out early to drive to the airport and meet Rosa at midday. I had parked in the hotel car park and deposited the keys at reception when I arrived, as requested and as the receptionist handed them back to me a man who was clearly upset approached the desk and said, "You won't get far with those". I asked him what he meant and he said that the car park was blocked, which was the reason for his apparent frustration. I didn't want to be late meeting Rosa, but before I could express my concern to the receptionist she smiled knowingly at me, shook her head almost imperceptibly and summoned the concierge to escort me. Then she turned to the man and asked him to wait while she telephoned the hotel manager.

The concierge opened the door for me and informed me that my car had been moved by hotel staff and was now in the upper-level car park, which had an alternative exit. When I asked why, he looked briefly across the foyer at the man and smiled mischievously before telling me the story;

The irate man was a traffic warden who usually parked his official vehicle in the hotel car park and the manager permitted this concession because there was plenty of space and she saw it as contributing to her civic duty. The warden had accepted this free parking for some years and over time he had started to leave his personal car there on a Saturday night, collecting it on Sunday morning. The hotel manager had also always turned a blind eye to this, however it seemed that the warden didn't view the gesture of goodwill as a reciprocal arrangement and a few weeks previously he had issued the manager's husband with an infringement notice whilst he had stopped on a yellow line for a few minutes outside the town hall to drop off a planning application. The application was to redevelop part of the lower-level car park, adding a second access to the existing single one, which was used for both entry and exit.

Annoyed about the parking fine, the hotel manager had arranged for construction work to start on the Sunday morning, agreeing with the construction firm that equipment deliveries would be easier in the lighter Sunday traffic. Guests who might be affected by the work were asked to leave their car keys at reception, as I had done and signs were displayed in the car park informing people that the car park was for the use of hotel guests only had been supplemented with warning notices that the car park would be closed for a week. Of course most people didn't read the notices anyway and the warden was no exception.

The contractor, as agreed with the manager, had turned up early and had not only deposited a shipping container in the car park but had also dug a two feet deep trench across the access road in preparation for installing an automated barrier. The warden's car was well and truly marooned!

I expect the contractor would have a method of bridging the trench so the warden probably got his car back eventually, but I would have liked to have been a fly on the wall during the conversation between him and the manager and I suspect the traffic warden who was too much of an idiot to recognise his previous good fortune probably never parked for free in that hotel car park again.

Not so Dumb Blonde

Sunday 11:35

I arrived at the airport nice and early and went to the coffee shop where Rosa and I had arranged to meet, ordered coffee and a doughnut and sat at a comfortable table to enjoy the Sunday Telegraph.

At the table next to mine were a smartly dressed guy of about thirty and a blonde woman maybe a couple of years younger whom looked like a couple, however from their conversation it transpired that although they were booked onto the same flight it had been delayed and they had actually only just met at the check-in desk. They had agreed to share a coffee, as young people often do when they first meet, but it was obvious to me that the guy was a little too keen to impress the girl and she had already started to lose interest because of his narcissistic demeanour.

The guy asked the blonde girl if she wanted to play a knowledge game to pass the time, but she declined politely and said she preferred to try and sleep for half an hour. She rested her head on her folded arms on the table but the guy persisted in explaining the rules to his game, which basically were that they would take turns to ask each other questions and if they didn't know the answers then they would pay a forfeit of one pound. The blonde again said she wasn't really interested and tried to resume her nap, but the guy was clearly intent on impressing her with his knowledge so he upped the stakes, saying that if she got a question wrong she would have to pay him one pound, but if he got one wrong he would pay her five pounds.

Either this bravado finally kindled the blonde girl's attention or perhaps she just figured he wasn't going to give up until she played, because she agreed to play the game for those stakes.

The guy asked the first question; "How far away from Earth is the moon?"

The blonde lass didn't say a word, but opened her purse, pulled out a pound coin and handed it to the guy. Then it was her turn and she asked the lad; "What goes up a hill with three legs and comes down with four?"

The guy looked puzzled and scratched his head. The blonde smiled lazily and returned her head to her previously comfy position to continue her nap. As she closed her eyes the chap furtively took out his smartphone and logged onto the airport WiFi to search the internet, but without success.

After fifteen minutes or so he woke the blonde up, took a five pound note from his pocket and handed it to her. She accepted the fiver graciously and thanked him, before returning to her nap. The guy was completely miffed and shook her gently to wake her up again then when she opened her eyes he asked; "So what's the answer? What does go up a hill with three legs and come down with four?"

Without saying a word, the blonde opened her purse, reached in and handed the guy another pound then put her head back on her folded arms and went back to sleep.

The idiot's face was a picture. I could hardly contain my laughter as he finally took the hint, picked up his bag and walked away, three pounds poorer.

Idiots at Dinner

Sunday 13.20

Rosa and I went to Danny Chu's, our favourite restaurant, for lunch. Danny is a superb chef and a wonderful host and we enjoy going to his restaurant on Sundays because business is usually quiet and we get to spend some time socialising with him. Danny is part Chinese but speaks very little Cantonese, so when a Chinese couple came in who spoke limited English the sensible thing to do would have been for Danny to call his wife, Tao, who is fluent, but for some reason he got himself entangled in trying to explain the menu and he slowly descended into the realms of stupid. The conversation went something like this:

Danny: "Good afternoon, have you decided what you would like?"

Customer: "Yes, we would like food please."

Both customer and Danny looked at each other awkwardly, until Danny realised that the customers weren't going to order without help and he needed to prompt them.

Danny: "OK, so what food would you like?"

The man looked at the menu and pointed at the lamb shanks then said, "I think I like this. This is steak, yes?"

Danny replied, "Oh, no, that's lamb shank,

it's like a small leg." He pointed at another part of the menu and said, "We have a steak just here, if you like?"

The customer continued to point at the lamb shank, saying, "So this is steak?"

Danny pointed at something else and said "No, no, this is steak. That is lamb."

The customer then asked, "So this ... what animal?"

Danny: "Pardon?"

Customer: "What animal this?"

Danny: "Oh. Sorry. That's lamb. Erm, sheep."

Customer: "Sheep?"

Danny: "Yes, sheep."

Customer: "Maaaaaaaa?"

Danny looked puzzled for a second or two, then realised that the customer was making a sheep noise. He looked relieved and said, "Yes, yes, baaaaa."

Then the customer smiled, pointed at the menu again and said "Ah yes, and this?"

Danny looked and said, "Steak. Cow."

The customer said, "Moooo?"

Danny replied "Yes, moooo!"

The customer then pointed to each item on the in turn and eventually Danny began to anticipate him and make the animal sounds before he did. Danny managed to keep a straight face, but his impressions were very funny and Rosa and I were in tears laughing.

The customer then pointed at the venison and asked, "And this? What animal, this?"

Danny replied, "That's venison, which is

deer."

Customer: "Deer? What is deer?"

Danny stopped in his tracks because he realised that he didn't have the faintest idea what noise a deer makes so he certainly couldn't reproduce it. He continued, "Erm … it's … erm … deer . I mean it's stag. You know, stag?" Approaching desperation Danny held his hands above his head in the shape of antlers and scuffed at the floor with his foot. The man looked puzzled for a moment, then seemed to have an epiphany and he exclaimed, "Ah … STAG!" He looked questioningly at his wife then back at Danny and said, "I … like … stag".

The tortured conversation was finally over and the customer did indeed end up with venison, which he seemed to enjoy very much. His wife appeared to be equally happy with her "Chicken cluck cluck".

Rosa and I laughed all the way home at the antics of our restaurateur friend, who isn't an idiot, but he certainly does a good impression of one!

From the moment I picked this book up until the moment I put it down I was convulsed with laughter. Someday I intend to read it!

Groucho Marx

Idiot Me

Sunday 16:00

After lunch we drove to my house, where Rosa planned to tidy up her work notes whilst I washed 800 miles of grime off the Jag. I parked on the drive and we went indoors, picking up five days' post on the way.

Rosa made coffee whilst I got my garage key, but on my way the pile of letters on the hall table captured my attention and as there was plenty of daylight left to wash the car I decided to sort the mail first. I put my key down and picked up the mail.

Like most people, I bin junk mail straight away and after an initial sort I had a handful of junk in one hand and some bills in the other. As I put the junk in the bin I thought it looked a bit full, so I decided to put the rubbish out. I put the bills on the worktop and as I did I noticed that the top one was a reminder from my electricity provider. Because I was going outside again anyway I thought I'd kill two birds with one stone and post the payment in the post box across the road, so I put the bin-liner down and went to the study for my chequebook. When I opened the desk drawer I realised I only had one cheque left, so I went back to the mail to check if my new chequebook had arrived.

Rosa had poured the coffee and I didn't

want it to get cold so I decided to pop it in the microwave.   As I crossed the kitchen I noticed the pot-plants on the window cill were drooping and I decided to change the water, so I went to the sink and as I was filling a jug I noticed I'd put my reading glasses on the worktop.   I decided to put them away, so I walked into the study with the jug in one hand and my glasses in the other and saw that I had left the television remote control in the study.   I knew we would be looking for it later so I decided to move the remote back into the lounge. As I went to pick it up, I spilled some water from the jug and cursed.   I headed back towards the kitchen for a cloth, tossing the remote onto a cushion on the sofa as I went.   I found myself standing in the hall, jug in one hand and an almost empty chequebook in the other, trying to remember what it was that I was going to do.

Rosa came and took the jug from me and led me to the sofa, where she made me sit and I fell asleep immediately.

I awoke later to find that the car wasn't washed, the bills remained unpaid, my coffee was still in the microwave, although Rosa had made a fresh pot, the flowers were still dying in bone-dry earth, I still only had one cheque in my chequebook and I had absolutely no idea where my garage key or the tv remote were.

I think I was just exhausted, but Rosa suggested I had spent so much time observing idiots that week that it was poetic justice and said it served me right for laughing at other people's misfortune.

Whoever was correct, every time I laugh at someone now, she quickly reminds me about my own idiot behaviour.

ABOUT THE AUTHOR

Henry Martin has spent half of his life working in the construction industry, starting "on the tools" and working his way up to become a qualified building surveyor, where writing reports for clients and technical articles for fellow professionals figured prominently in his work. He has a respectable catalogue of published work, although he is always quick to point out that it has a strong technical and / or legal bias and is therefore of little interest to the "man on the Clapham omnibus".

Of course there are only so many words that can be written about the crushing strength of concrete or the moment of shear in carbon steel and Henry has decided to try and expand his writing to appeal to a wider audience than architects, surveyors and engineers. This anthology started out as an exercise in planning a work of fiction, however it rapidly took on an identity which we felt was worthy of publication on its own merit.

We hope you enjoyed it.

Made in the USA
Charleston, SC
04 July 2015